How to Obey Your Cat

GRAZIA VALCI

How to Obey Your Cat

Translated from Italian by Angie McNee

GREMESE

Original title: Come Ubbidire al Gatto

Translation revised by: Shula Atil Curto

Illustrations: Yolanda Zerboni

Cover by: apostoli & maggi – Rome

Photocomposition and photoprinting:
Graphic Art 6 s.r.l. – Rome

Printed by:
C.S.R. – Rome

Copyright GREMESE
2001 © E.G.E. s.r.l. – Rome

Introduction

The first question we must ask ourselves is: should we obey, or are we to be obeyed? All domesticated animals end up obeying man, one way or another. All domesticated animals except for the cat, that is.

Should His Majesty, our feline friend, decide that he cannot be bothered with you, flattery will get you nowhere, and nor will threats. Quite the contrary. A smack is more likely to cause him to raise his paw, claws outstretched, or even to wail loudly, as if he were being skinned alive. True, it is usually the female cat in search of a bit of male company who is the one making all the noise, but the protests of the male cat will really stop you in your tracks. His piercing cries of **rrrooahhaha**, or **mahahahaaah**, are bewildering, agonizing and even heartrending. They often cause the worried owner considerable concern, that his feline friend is ill, or has eaten something disagreeable. He might even harbor the suspicion that it was all his fault, for trying to force his four-legged friend to obey him.

The outcome is inevitable. Make the cat obey? Quite the opposite! It is you who must obey the cat, if you are to avoid worrying all day long, as you listen to those cries, that perhaps you should be less strict with the poor little creature, who only wants to be loved, after all. Purring contentedly, your furry friend takes full advantage of your remorse in order to get his own way.

This little book has been written to help all those who find it impossible to stand firm, and continually find themselves giving in to their cat's whims.

However, it is not intended as an instruction manual to get your cat jumping through hoops of fire. Neither is it for prospective lion-tamers, but for those who simply desire to get along with their feline companions. Nor is it intended as a beginners' guide to a kind of DIY psycho-ethological pedagogy, or a recipe book with instructions such as: *"take one cat, and cook slowly in a bain-marie"*, *à la* Chantilly cream.

Rather, it is a collection of observations made by the author about her own pet cats, and others she has known, and of tales told by friends and relatives, who are cat-lovers like herself. A collection of short stories and anecdotes, each one concluding with a piece of advice. Well-grounded? Misconceived? The author leaves it up to you to decide.

The independent cat

As all two-legged cat-lovers are aware – and, we believe, other animals are also aware – the cat is an independent, self-reliant creature, in complete control not only of himself, but also of the human being who believes himself or herself to be the boss.

This, and other characteristics, distinguish him from the dog, who is happy to sit at man's feet, content with being stroked, and eager to submit.

Nor is the cat like the donkey who, as the saying goes, allows himself to be led wherever his master wishes.

Or the horse, whose friendship for man is substantiated in tales, old and new, describing acts of devotion, love and even bravery.

A well-known Italian doctor, a friend of the author, once told a story about his horse and its colt. He was quite out of sorts one day, and the two horses not only showed affection towards him, but even expressed real understanding. He was sitting on the fence which encircled the paddock where the mare and her colt lived; he was extremely disgruntled, and in no mood for stroking his two animals. The colt came up to him, but the doctor irritably pushed him away. Then the mare came too, and gently laid her nose on his shoulder, encouraging her colt to do the same. What could he do, except feel sorry for having been so harsh?

And so to the cat. In vain has the human tried to get the cat to come along on walks with him. He has tried to make his friend wear fancy, or even elegant leashes, to stop him from running off. The cat detests this, as he hates being restrained; he wants to be free to choose what he is going to do, and whether or not to go along with his human. The cat wants to be able to accompany him spontaneously, of his own free will, even dictating which way they will go.

Many humans claim that their cat absolutely refuses to get into one of those travelling cages, causing no end of difficulties whenever they have to go away. If it is only a matter of a few days, some people prefer to leave their stubborn feline friend at home, supplied with plenty of water, food and clean litter in the litter-tray. But what if you are going away for more than a few days? It is not always possible to comply with your cat's desire to have an obliging friend keep an eye on him for a while.

Even Memeo, Picò, Paco, Polly, Arthur and Tarzan, the protagonists of many of the episodes described in the following pages, were rebellious at first. But after a while we only had to say: "Come on, into the basket, we're going out", and they would grudgingly put up with their temporary imprisonment.

Polly is the only one who never made a lot of fuss, in other words she never scuttled under a low bed in order to craftily thwart attempts to catch her. She put up with the travelling cage and the inevitable car journey which came with it, as long as it was placed between Memeo's basket and one of the human passengers, who was obviously not in a travelling cage, albeit imprisoned by the seatbelt.

Helpful advice: 1) It is, of course, perfectly right that every living creature's claim to freedom should be respected, including the cat's. But how can we safeguard an animal's desperate need for freedom in our chaotic cities, which are choked with traffic, and permeated with indifference, or within a society lacking in fundamental values?

There are many roadside notices in France, particularly on those roads running through the so-called green belt areas, reminding drivers that this is an unfenced area, and that there may be animals on the road ahead. But there will always be the same broken little bodies lying on the tarmac. And so it may seem justifiable to restrain such precarious freedom, for the sake of survival, trying nonetheless to keep these restraints to a minimum.

2) There is no need to shout at your four-legged friend in order to force him into the travelling cage. Greater success will be achieved with gentle persuasion. Cats detest shouting and screaming, and will only do so themselves in the presence of an adversary. They are therefore completely baffled

when their human shouts, and seem to be asking themselves, "Has he perhaps suddenly become an enemy?" Prior to travelling, it is an excellent ploy to leave the basket around, so that the cat becomes used to it and, his suspicions thus allayed, is no longer so reluctant to get into it.

How difficult the cat can be!

Paco, our ginger tomcat, was sitting on the bed one day, looking a bit depressed, with his paws tucked under his body, a sure sign of discomfort, the experts claim. The human touched him gently along his sides, and on his nose, as all the books advise. But that was all that could be done, because Paco has a naturally irascible nature. Imagine what he is like when he really feels unwell! We were visiting friends in the country at the time, and there was a doctor amongst us who, having quite correctly lectured us on the differences between human medicine and veterinary science, agreed to take a quick look at our 'patient'.

"Well", he advised, "I would just treat him like a child who has eaten too much. Don't give him any food at all today, it won't do any harm." And, pointing at Paco's dish full of goodies, he continued, "you can start by getting rid of that." Paco, the sneaky cat, obviously understood this diagnosis, and darted over to his dish, polishing off the lot before his human had the chance to carry out the doctor's orders. He then curled up on the bed once again, purring contentedly, and stopped complaining that he was out of sorts from that moment on.

Paco is Picò's "cousin-in law", one might say, as they are not actually related. They had been adopted by two families who were related by marriage. Paco was rescued as a tiny kitten from the side of a busy city street; Picò, a little older, was found in the garden of our holiday home by the sea. Both of them were in an extremely bad way.

You would think, from their characters, that they were actually related, however.

Every cat has a distinct personality. There are some who are extremely haughty, and others who are more easy-going; some might be malicious, others a little timid. As with all living creatures, there is no such thing as a "typical" cat. Even plants differ from one other. The variations might be slight, but nonetheless they really count.

There is the cat who will bear a grudge against his owner if he happens to have been away from home too long, or has delayed his return, in other words has appeared later than expected. The cat will punish him by staying away from the bed, or vigorously demanding more room on the armchair on which they usually settle down together quite happily.

Then there is the cat who tries to assert his right to go out, even though, for his own safety, he is not allowed to do so, and even if, were the front door to actually close behind him, he would howl desperately to be let back inside.

Yes, cats can be really difficult. Those of us who share our lives with a cat know a little bit about this, and have learned to accept the fact that, "If your four-legged friend has decided to do something against your wishes, you might as well just let him get on with it." (see *The impertinent cat*).

Nevertheless, who does the cat turn to when his dish is empty, if not the human?

Once, when Polly tried to scratch her chin, she

managed to get a claw caught in her collar. If she had tried to pull it free, she would have strangled herself. So she waited patiently for someone to find her. With gentle reassurances, she was released without so much as a struggle, even though generally she hated being touched.

Helpful advice: 1) The incident regarding Paco's stomach-ache taught us that we could only make the cat obey by being devious. It is an excellent idea if, every now and then, it is you who are the disobedient one!

2) If the cat is ensconced beneath a shrub in the garden, or hidden inside a large flowerpot on the terrace, and you want him back in the house (see *What Did the Cat Say?* by Grazia Valci, published by Gremese), it is no good quietly calling to him, or even firmly ordering him back inside, as he will pretend not to understand. Even if it begins to rain, he will obstinately stay put, even though he hates getting wet, just so he does not have to do what the human wants. On the other hand, if he lets you pick him up and carry him back to the house, it is

because he has decided that he has had enough fresh air and freedom.

3) Does your cat terrify you by using the washing line as a tightrope, stretched from one window to another some fifteen meters above the courtyard? If you want to avoid a heart-attack, just close the window! Before he starts showing you how clever he is.

The Spartan

Fortunately, the cat's needs are few. Although he prefers to lounge about on the sofa rather than sit on a marble or tiled floor (**mmmaah** – brr, that's cold!), the 'high and mighty' image with which he is sometimes portrayed is not altogether justified. Nor is it justified to see him as a sort of four-legged despot just because he sleeps a lot! True, he does sleep a lot, but only with one eye closed. He may appear to be asleep for long periods of time, but he always has one eye open. His Majesty the cat never completely abandons himself to the land of nod, part of him is always alert. Curled up in his favorite position in the corner, the cat makes sure he has a comfy bed, and adequate protection from any unexpected interruptions.

The cat's needs are indeed few, as he is perfectly content with just a little food and his catnaps. A stray cat can get by on even less, and has few pretensions. He survives on the food he comes across whilst rummaging about in an open trash can, or by catching small lizards and unwary birds (the cat does not find mice very tasty, and will only eat one when 'starving hungry', as they say). The stray cat will sleep wherever he can, beneath a bush, or next to a wall warmed by the sun.

If a pet cat suddenly finds himself, whether intentionally or unintentionally, free but homeless, he will have a tough time scraping through, and even if he does he will have learnt that freedom has a high price. And if he has been subjected, for convenience's sake, to that uncivilized but extremely common practice of neutering, the risks he runs are even greater.

Because of the busy lives we are forced to lead nowadays, it is precisely because the cat asks for so little that we prefer him as a pet to a dog.

The famous Picò (see above-mentioned *What Did the Cat Say?*) was homeless for some four months when he was still a kitten, and obviously suffered some trauma during this brief spell of freedom, which still gives him nightmares. He fights, hisses, and unsheathes his claws at an imaginary attacker, whom he will never get the chance to discuss with an analyst. Because, just like all the others of his kind, he is uncommunicative.

By the way, when *does* a cat sleep? It is simply not true that he sleeps for at least seventeen hours a day. And as he is even wary of his own shadow, he never allows himself to fall into a deep sleep, but is always ready to flee at the slightest noise which could signal danger.

In any case, the cat comes fourth on the following list of animals which sleep a great deal:

   1) the koala sleeps for twenty-two hours a day;

   2) the sloth sleeps for twenty hours;

   3) the armadillo and the opossum sleep for nineteen hours;

   4) the cat sleeps for a maximum of nineteen hours, although recent research indicates that he actually sleeps for less, around thirteen hours;

   5) the lemur sleeps for sixteen hours;

   6) the hamster and the squirrel sleep for fourteen hours;

   7) the pig sleeps for thirteen hours;

8) the ant-eater sleeps for twelve hours.

Other animals, apart from those which hibernate during the winter, sleep the same number of hours, on average, as humans.

Helpful advice: 1) If the cat chooses the crook of your arm as a good place to settle down, quickly turn him over as soon as he appears to be asleep. In this way, you will ensure that your arm does not get caught up in the crossfire during any somnambulistic scuffles. His Majesty the cat will occasionally fall into a deep sleep, and has even been known to snore. Acquaintances of ours have mistaken Picò's snoring for that of a human.

2) Does your cat want to explore the neighborhood? Let him go, but remember there is no surer way of getting him to change his mind than the sound of the shutters coming down, barring his entry back into the house, or the sound of the door closing behind him. He is quite capable of throwing himself against the unexpected obstacle, wailing louder than Niobe. A sneaky way, you will agree, of getting him to return to the peace and calm of the house.

Cats and politics

If the cat were into politics, to which party would he belong? Would he be a conservative? Quite possibly, as his ancestry dictates that he is extremely reluctant to try anything new, whether for reasons of laziness or expedience. However, as we saw in *The independent cat*, he would be an independent conservative, a little antagonistic towards the working classes. In fact, the cat is generally mistrustful of tradesmen, particularly when they bring the bizarre tools of their trade with them in an enormous bag. Tools which get thrown down with a great clatter, startling His Majesty as he lies sleeping on the chair. Nor can they tolerate cleaning ladies, particularly when armed with a vacuum cleaner, or even just a broom. Our four-legged friend is not only an independent conservative, but also something of a snob. However, he does have an instinctive, hereditary dislike of the traditional equipment of his one-time friend, the witch. There are two possible reasons for this aversion: one related to his recollection of how dearly he paid for that dispassionate friendship a couple of centuries ago; and the other due to the fact that the broom is no longer used by the witch, who would never have actually turned this utensil on him, but by touchy housewives who resent the cat's presence in their kitchens.

Even our ginger tomcat, Picò, exhibits unequivocal antagonism when it comes to cleaning sprees. When our Filipino helper has to give the kitchen or the terrace a good clean on Thursday afternoons, Picò becomes downright disobedient, and makes repeated attempts to hinder the intruder, each one more amusing than the last, hiding the dusters, or attacking the packets of detergent. We suspect that he may even be planning to launch an attack on the Filipino's short, black pigtail. And when we finally succeed in making him abandon his crusade, he hides away in the furthest bedroom, fuming and fussing.

Although he detests all household electrical appliances, he does love curling up on top of the pile of clean washing which has just been taken off the clothes dryer, and is waiting to be ironed.

Helpful advice: In order to prevent our four-legged friend the discomfort of having to watch a stranger wandering around "his" house, we actually shut the cat in the room where he would seek refuge anyway, before the cleaner arrives. This also ensures that he does not impulsively run off, as we once saw a large black and white cat do. The cat used to sit quietly on the mezzanine window sill each day. One morning, perhaps startled by the plumber, who had been called in to fix a leak by the owner of the house – an elderly lady, who was very fond of her cat – the frightened animal took a feline leap into the street below. The elderly lady was completely distraught, and went down on her hands and knees to try and persuade her pet to come out from beneath a car parked nearby. It was the first time we heard a cat-owner calling to her four-legged friend: "Come to Granny, come on". Granny! You usually hear women saying to their pets, "Come to Mummy"!

The affectionate cat

Cats know how to love. The cat loves his own kind, but loves his human best of all.

There was a female cat that used to live next door to us in town, who could not have kittens as she had been neutered, and so she adopted a little stray. The cat would always rush to her protégé's rescue, whenever anyone dared to scold her.

We are well aware that nothing could be further from the truth than to say that our four-legged friend loves his home, but is indifferent towards everyone who lives there. Dear old Memeo, who has been peacefully at rest beneath the pine tree in the garden of our holiday home by the sea for some years now, used to amaze those who did not know him, or people who, being unacquainted with cats, believed that the cat loves only himself, when he climbed up on to one of his human's shoulders staying there for hours, draped around her neck like a fur boa; or when he hugged his two-legged friend as she slept, quietly watching over her, but without disturbing her.

By the way, just to avoid any possible injunctions, I should mention that Memeo was laid to rest prior to the recent law prohibiting such burials on private land.

Two friends of ours – a husband and wife, both well-known archaeologists living in Rome – adopted Messalina. Or rather, as we are talking about a cat, perhaps we should say that they were adopted by Messalina.

Messalina, a pale gray cat, took shelter under their porch one stormy evening. They took her inside, gave her something to warm her up, and let her settle down between them. The cat took an immediate liking to the man, and often reacted jealously – not only towards his wife, who had rescued her in her hour of need, but also towards the large reference books which he placed on a lectern in order to consult them more easily. Messalina used to push the lectern over, brushing past it and knocking it with her shoulder. Whenever her human caught her doing this, and scolded her, she always got him to forgive her by rubbing against his legs, and purring loudly, just like a motorbike coming to life. Her subterfuge was not so much aimed at obtaining forgiveness, as reminding her owner that *she* deserved to be the center of attention, and making sure that he was distracted from all that reading which took his attention away from her.

Helpful advice: 1) Never misinterpret your feline friend's show of affection as craftiness, as the cat is completely sincere in his devotion, and should be given the benefit of the doubt.

2) Never believe that your cat is unique, in terms of intelligence, or that his behavior is somehow exceptional compared with other cats.

Even Memeo, Polly, Picò, Paco, Arthur, Tarzan, Messalina, and Bigpuss – who is not mentioned very often, as she was part of the author's teenage years (and therefore almost prehistoric!) – even they were, and are, just ordinary cats. However, their funny little ways, their reactions to certain situations, their whims and creativity, have all contributed, and continue to contribute, towards making the cat an enchanting, amusing, but disobedient, companion. Be reasonable, however, you have to obey your cat. Do not feel bad about it. If nothing else, just back down gracefully.

The hypersensitive cat

We used to own a dog – an extremely irritable, hypersensitive fox terrier, who would go for anyone who dared laugh at him. Our family used to think that only dogs were irascible, but we soon discovered that cats can be touchy, too. We have had generations and families of cats at our home, and every single one of them proved to be hypersensitive, in one way or another. They really take it to heart if you pretend not to understand what they are saying when they create such a fuss, using the full range of 'cat talk', that only the most dull-witted human would not comprehend what they wanted. When they finally realize that you are not going to do anything, and that you really did not understand what they were saying, they will clarify the situation by physically guiding you towards the window which they want opened, or to the empty dish which should be filled, or the cat litter which needs cleaning.

Picò, who often appears in this book because he is

the ginger tomcat who happily lives with us at present, gets very cross with us when we do not carry out his wishes, or ignore his needs. He never scratches us, thank goodness, nor does he hiss or sigh, but he punishes us instead by ignoring us, sometimes for an hour or more, and occasionally up to three days! He turns his nose up at the delicious snacks which are proffered, partly because he is no connoisseur; he wriggles away from anyone who tries to stroke him, and obstinately retreats from the family circle, where he generally loves being the center of attention.

Helpful advice: 1) Does your four-legged friend ignore all your attempts to get him to stop doing certain things, of which you disapprove? It is no good lecturing him about how disgraceful his stubbornness is. Let him have his own way. Do not worry that he might get up to mischief. Just act as if nothing is wrong, and he will not get into any bother at all. He is not stupid. Ignore him completely, and you will notice how his behavior changes. He cannot bear to be ignored, and will become extremely offended. Just give as good as you get.

The unresponsive cat

A dog will watch your every move, eagerly waiting for you to notice him or stroke him. The cat is completely different. And yet, his nonchalance is not altogether genuine. How can he be nonchalant, when he is dominated by curiosity? He will be watching your every move from beneath closed eyes, with the same interest as a dog. He will do it surreptitiously, however, and is not actually waiting for his two-legged companion to pay him some attention. Rather, it is just so that he can keep an eye on what is happening.

There are many different reasons why your cat will pretend to be indifferent: a) he wants to punish you, as we explained previously (see *The hypersensitive cat*); b) he would rather not be bothered with your cajoling; c) he has got something more important to do, such as catching a lizard, or pretending to be a butterfly.

If it were not for the fact that the cat occasionally gives us a bit of a scare when we cannot find him, it would be amusing to note how successfully he is able to hide himself away.

   "He was right here a moment ago", you say, pointing towards the open door. "Perhaps he got out when we weren't looking." And you become more and more convinced that he has gone for good. You think of all the fliers you have been given by other cat-owners who have lost their pets, and all the posters you have seen pinned to trees, or stuck up in shop windows: "Generous reward for information about a missing cat, tawny-colored with white paws, answering to the name of Queen Taitù..." As if the cat knew how to pronounce its own name! They may actually know how to say their name, but this would be in 'cat talk', which humans cannot speak. When the cat realizes how worried you are, then he will guide you towards his hiding place. How does he do this? Don't laugh when I tell you, as it really does happen: with the power of thought. You will see a strange light in his beautiful eyes, gazing at you, a sort of telepathic gleam which searched for you and drew you to him.

Helpful advice: Do not be fooled if he appears to be lost in a brightly-colored dream world whilst you are speaking to him. He is merely being impudent. If he wants to be left alone, it simply means that he finds your affection disagreeable at that particular moment. When he is fed up with being aloof, he will emerge once again from his hiding place, or else he will call out to you. Then you can pay him back by taking no notice of him! As they say, patience wins out in the end!

The cat's curiosity

You may come back home with a parcel, or carrying a suitcase because you have been away, or possibly just a shopping bag. You know, of course, that you will have to contend with your cat's shameless curiosity. Your four-legged friend will plead with you, and weave around you until he gets you to open the suitcase or the parcel. Or else he will insolently thrust his nose into your shopping bag. When a cat finds an envelope, box, or any other container which is interesting enough to be tempting, there are several things which he may do: a) jump straight into it. This is particularly the case with large bags or suitcases, as he can easily fit in, with just the top of his head sticking out so that he can keep watch for anything unexpected; b) if the bag is too full, he will briskly set about emptying it, using his two front paws. This almost always means that he will get into trouble, particularly if there is foodstuff in the bag. Have you ever seen a cat chasing after an egg as it rolls off the table? And when it falls on to the floor, have you noticed how he peers over the edge and stares, enthralled, at the yellow mess?

"**Mowmmah**". This is not only a question, but also a declaration of what he intends to do, driven on by his insatiable curiosity; c) if it is a suitcase which is packed and ready to go, there is always a chance that you may take along an extra traveler – a stowaway.

"**Mowmmah**", Memeo used to declare, just before climbing up a tree, attracted by the rustling of the branches, or by the swaying movements of a yellow wagtail. And once he was up the tree, we then had to use all the tricks in the book to persuade him to come down again. It may have been that, just like all cats, the intrepid Memeo was scared to come down head first. So he used to wait until we had gone away to do something else, at which point he would lower himself down the trunk, bottom first, looking a little ridiculous, and probably feeling completely mortified.

Helpful advice: 1) Just go along with your curious cat, as long as he is not going to do any irreparable damage, even if it means you have to waste a bit of time doing so. It is fun to watch a cat thoroughly investigating the contents of a bag, with his whiskers twitching. He sniffs at something, moves on, pauses a moment, goes back and sniffs at it again, walks around the item that interests him, and rubs his head against the bag's handles.

If you want to have a good night's sleep after returning from a trip, make sure you take the time to unpack your suitcase and put it safely away, even if you are really tired. Otherwise, you will be awoken by the racket your cat makes as he pushes the suitcase all around the house, crashing, one wonders whether intentionally, against doors and furniture.

2) As for other predicaments your four-legged friend may get himself into trying to satisfy his curiosity, you must act as you think best, as we cannot really give any further advice on this. As they say, everyone is capable of making his own mistakes!

The dignified cat

Whereas the dog will let you do whatever you want to him, the cat will not. The cat will not let you put a coat and hat on him, unlike the dog. The cat tolerates cold weather, and avoids the rain whenever possible. He will even stoically, quietly, put up with being ill, at times. A dog will allow himself to be taken along on a lead. People have tried, and failed, to do so with the cat.

Look how elegantly the cat sits and waits for things to happen. You decide to read the new label on his favorite cat food, for example. But His Majesty the cat will never tell you how hungry he is, for goodness' sake! He will watch your every move, maintaining his dignity and restraint. If hunger starts to get the better of him, he will remind you with a quiet but unequivocal **marammamow**.

His Majesty the cat. He truly believes himself to be of royal lineage. How can we say that he is not, when his ancestors were to be found populating the courts of the Pharaohs and the Quirites allowed them to ride on the triumphal chariots? Then there were the difficult years, of course, when they were burned along with their owners, the reputed witches. Yet they never lost their dignity. Even when persecuted, the cat maintains his wonderfully majestic attitude. And although he detests water, he is always extremely clean. The cat will wash himself several times a day with his rough little tongue, and will even try to lick the makeup off his human's face.

Nowadays, in Italy, the cat is protected by law (281/91), and deservedly so. Many communities, both large and small, have set up official bodies for the protection of animal rights. These organizations work together with animal rights groups, universities, and research laboratories. Through the work carried out by these groups, people have even learned to respect feral cats (the term "stray" is, quite rightly, no longer used). The cities which are home to the largest number of feral cats are Rome and Milan. Rome is actually referred to as the city of the cat, which is wholly justified, considering the number of times an archeological dig has uncovered his ancestor's remains. There are about 170,000 individual groups of cats in Rome; of which there are some 480 groups protected both by the ASL Organization and by the Society for Animal Rights. There are over 200,000 pet cats in Rome, with similar numbers in Milan and Turin. Cats are loved all over America, Europe and the Far East. In the Netherlands and Germany we have visited feline colonies alongside some of the canal routes, where feral cats are well fed and cared for.

Helpful advice: 1) Don't bother your four-legged friend when he is sitting quietly. Admire him from afar, and leave him in peace, but do not try and stroke him. You could even take a photograph of him. The cat loves posing for a picture, and is an ideal subject, responding well to those who enjoy using zoom lenses and flash photography.

2) If you find that your cat gets under your feet, getting in the way, or even causing you to trip, just be careful. Do not try and make him go away, but simply avoid him. You will find that it is quite easy to do so.

Sociable or unsociable?

The cat generally gets along with his human house mates, whether he is living with them out of true friendship, or out of necessity. However, his relationship with other cats, or with other animals, is not so straightforward. The relationship between a cat and a German Shepherd, for example, does have certain problems. But even the cat's relationship with others of his kind is not without difficulties. Picò, usually so amiable, snarls and hisses "**fccchhh, rrrooahhahah**" like a howling gale whenever he sees the outline of one of the neighborhood cats through the glass panes which separate our terrace from next door. This causes the large, friendly dog next door to join in as well. His low pitched barking then sets off a small mongrel who lives on the second floor, and who loves to join in the affray, even though he has no idea what it is all about.

The cat will also sometimes be unsociable with people who are not part of his close circle of acquaintances. And when he seems to be afraid of people, it is likely he has learned to fear them, at his cost.

Memeo the "Great", the gray cat who lived with us for sixteen years, always used to run away from people he did not know. He seemed to sense that it was not one of the family as soon as the doorbell went. But he had never been badly treated by anyone, unlike Polly, the cat who shared her home, food and our love with him for eleven years.

In spite of his enforced impotence, the gray was a real philanderer with the ladies, except for Polly, whose coat was multi-colored, whereas Memeo preferred female cats with coats of a single color. "**Ohhohoo**", he would purr, making sure that we gave some of his food to the intruder and watching her admiringly as she ate. He would have shared his favorite chair with her as well, if we had let him. One day, Polly got tired of this, finding it extremely insulting, and badly beat up one of the intruders.

After this, Memeo ceased his philandering, and the other female cats only had to see our Polly, and off they ran.

It is amusing to see how our ginger tomcat reacts to Brutus, a mynah bird owned by a nephew of ours, who leaves him with us when he has to go away on business or on holiday. The mynah bird has learned how to say, "hello", and "who's that", as well as his owner's name. At first, Picò approached the bird boldly, perhaps looking forward to a tasty morsel. But Brutus halted him in his tracks with a loud, distinctly human-sounding, "hello". The cat halted, retreated and then turned his back on this strange creature. After he had regained his composure, he haughtily strode off. Now, every time that he goes near the large cage and Brutus calls out to him, he knowingly replies with a "**mmow**", watching the mynah bird for a while, but keeping his distance. He is clearly puzzled by the fact that the bird, who is obviously inferior to himself, knows how to talk like a human.

Memeo did not meet Brutus, but he did come across many other small birds. He never harmed any of them, taking heed of the strict "don't you touch it", which was reiterated each time he set off, tail held low, to investigate a baby bird which had fallen out of its nest. In fact, he would accompany his human and together they would try to catch the bird and put it back in the tree.

Whenever he managed to catch a mouse – one of the small, brown mice found in the countryside – he would place it at his human's feet. Was this meant as a gift, or just proof of how clever he was? It would be nice to believe that he was presenting us with a trophy, just like the paws that have been removed from the poor fox are presented to the most distinguished lady after a day of hunting.

Just as our gray cat did during his time with us, Picò also enjoys holding long conversations with the humans in the family (see *What did the cat say?*). It was, and is, highly amusing to listen to these discussions.

"**Gur gur gur**", says our four-legged friend, as he turns around two or three times, trying to find the most comfortable spot on the sofa.

"Umm", comments his two-legged friend, "but make sure you don't take up all the room, and don't you dare sit on my newspaper."

"**Fffeefffeeoo**", the cat responds.

"I love you, too," says the human, turning back to her book.

"**Gur ron gur ron**", continues our four-legged friend.

"You're making so much fuss", his companion complains, "that I'm just going to leave you to it in a minute."

Helpful advice: 1) There is nothing you can do. Once a cat has taken a dislike to another cat, it is pointless to try and keep the peace. The only thing you can do is to keep them apart, at least until they get used to one another.

2) If a cat is scared of certain people, it is a good idea to find out why and make sure they do not meet. Usually, the cat's instinct will be proved correct, and his mistrust should encourage his owner to be wary of strangers, or those he does not know very well.

The guard cat

This chapter echoes what we were saying earlier about feline instinct with regard to strangers. Just like the dog, the cat will guard, defend and protect his home, and the humans who live there.

As we have said, each time the doorbell went, our old gray cat seemed to expect to see a stranger, or someone he disliked. And so, with a tremendous leap, he would jump on top of a cupboard, from where he could see the entrance hall, and he would watch every movement made by the intruder. When, after a moment or two, he realized that it made us laugh, he took full advantage of the situation and would perform his acrobatic leap even when the intruders were only our nephews and nieces, who found his tricks highly amusing (see *The playful cat*). On a couple of occasions, however, his threatening behavior did actually discourage an intruder.

And we should not forget to acknowledge the cat's

merits in keeping away such creatures as mice, vicious insects and snakes.

Picò catches wasps and mosquitoes. It is better that he eliminates them rather than certain other chemical exterminators.

Helpful advice: Any suggestions? Should we stop our four-legged friend from doing something which, all in all, may help to keep us safe? The cat who hisses at a stranger should not be scolded. He is just doing his job. It is up to us to make sure that his heroic actions do not get out of hand. Both the cat and the unfortunate person who is the object of his arbitrary suspicion should be reassured, and also kept apart!

The honest cat

An honest cat? Hmm. It would seem that our four-legged friend is amongst those creatures which are not renowned for their honesty. In fact, it would seem that the cat has the reputation of being something of a thief. There are thousands of stories which tell of the cat stealing sausages, just like a dog, or pilfering, like the magpie. But there are some important differences which should be noted.

Memeo never stole because he needed food, as he always had plenty. He occasionally stole because he wanted to annoy his humans who, in his opinion, were neglecting him. Or he would steal to please a friend, particularly if it was a female. For Tarzan, who was a great pal of his, he even risked snatching a slice of roast meat. On another occasion, after several attempts to get his humans to give one of his female friends some of his very best food, when his demands were ignored, he just helped himself.

Bigpuss, who – as we have already mentioned – is part of the author's childhood memories, stole a piece of meat from the saucepan, in order to please a dog. A dog, of all things....he must have led her to believe that he was extremely hungry.

Picò never steals. He merely expects food, and so always gets fed.

It is usually female cats who are more likely to steal, for a very good reason. The need to find food any way they can, even by stealing it, is an age-old habit, in order to feed their young. So, even if they have never had kittens, they will steal and then gorge themselves, in response to the maternal instincts which drive them.

Helpful advice: All in all, the preferable alternative are the tactics adopted by Picò who, having strong belief in his humans' compliance, and in his own powers of persuasion, never has to resort to illicit means in order to get what he wants. This is good advice for both cats and humans.

The impertinent cat

If your cat is cheeky, or behaves in a completely disgraceful manner, it is because he is trying to get his own back. He probably had a wonderful plan in mind, which his human, not realizing what was going on, inadvertently ruined. When our ginger tomcat decides that he wants some fresh air, he will not listen to reason, whatever time it may be. We might be just about to have a bath, or to go out on an urgent errand, or it might be raining, and it would be better for him not to go out on the terrace in the wet weather, but he will still pace up and down in front of the door, almost shrieking. If we fail to carry out his wishes, and do not open the terrace door immediately, he will head towards the best carpet to use as a scratching post.

We believe that, using channels of communication, not yet fully understood, cats refer to a kind of feline handbook in order to make their two-legged friend do exactly what they want, for example:

1) If your humans do not get out of bed when you are wide awake already, just caterwaul your disapproval. Caterwaul loudly, and then even louder!

2) If you do not wat to go back to sleep and they try to make you, open the wardrobe door and, before climbing in, carefully pull out all the clean, ironed clothes and throw them into the middle of the room.

3) If they leave your dish half-empty, and you want to make it perfectly clear that leftovers are not to your liking, jump up on to the bathroom shelf, where all their best bottles and vases are lined up, and sweep them right off with your paw. And if you get hungry in the middle of the night, and you cannot find anything to eat, then just pick up your dish – which they will have left empty, so that you will not be able to spread cat biscuits all over the house for fun – and take it to the foot of the bed, where you should bang it on the floor. Ensure that it makes a lot of noise!

4) If they do not wake up, jump up on to the chest of drawers, or the dressing table, or anything on which

they keep what you understand to be their most precious things, pick out a few of them, and push them over the edge. If you come across a pair of stockings, all nice and clean for the following day, push them under the chest of drawers. Hide the umbrella cover, or a pair of gloves, under the carpet. You will think of plenty of other things to do, I am sure.

5) If she is in the bathroom, messing about with various bottles, jugs and tubes, and does not seem to realize your need to go out and enjoy the beautiful spring day, grab hold of her hairbrush, and then lead her in a merry dance all through the house, making sure she bumps into the doors.

6) If they have invited guests for dinner – you can tell by the fact that they are using the best china, and that there are flowers in the middle of the table – and you could do without all the commotion at that particular moment, just jump up on to the tablecloth and eat the green stuff that has been put in with the flowers. Should the vase tip over, spilling water all over the tablecloth, scuttle off before you are discovered and punished.

7) If you want the guests to leave as soon as possible, so that the house is nice and quiet again, curl up on their coats and make sure that they get covered in fur. In particular, spend lots of time on the coats which belong to the people who claim they are allergic to cats. If this does not get rid of the invaders, pace up and down nearby, twitching your tail from side to side, and stare at them intently until they notice you. Then turn and walk slowly towards the door. If this does not get them moving, go back to where they are seated and do it all over again, until they finally get the message.

8) If the chatter in the living-room looks as if it will continue for hours, it is time to reclaim your favorite chair. However, you must be clever and subtle about this, first of all settling down near to the person who is sitting in your favorite spot. Then, gradually force him towards the edge, until it becomes obvious what you want, and the person in question has to take his tail-less rump elsewhere.

9) When you are curled up beneath the dwarf palm, enjoying the cool shade, and hidden from

view, and you hear them calling because they want to know where you are, defend your privacy by ignoring them, and just let them carry on shouting. They will find you eventually, but not before you have given them a bit of a scare, which is not such a bad thing.

10) If your human is engrossed in his newspaper, instead of realizing that you want some fuss, just grab that horrible paper in your mouth and chew it up.

You should never let them stop you doing exactly what you want. Unless... Unless they tell you off in a really heartfelt tone of voice, accusing you of all manner of vandalism.

Helpful advice: We do not really know what the best advice is in these circumstances, as we too are horrified, and completely powerless to do anything, when our cat behaves in such an appalling way.

1) Gently hold him and threaten him with a newspaper, or any type of paper. It seems that the cat just cannot bear the noise this makes.

2) Or perhaps you could vent your anger by calling

your cheeky cat as many insulting names as you can think of. This can be very effective, as the cat is extremely sensitive.

It might even be sensible just to give in completely, particularly as the cat is more than capable of just walking away from whatever it was he seemed to want more than anything else a moment ago, once he is fed up with it, and delight you by coming over and butting you gently, as if nothing had happened.

3) It is extremely tempting just to let him have his own way, and allow him out on to the terrace, or into the garden, when it is pouring with rain. We have done it ourselves, even though it means cleaning up his muddy footprints from the floor and carpets. We have even had a good laugh as he comes back in, soaking wet and dejected. We just dry him off, rubbing him vigorously with a towel, in spite of his protests, thus getting our own back.

4) As for the newspaper, which continually gets ripped to shreds, we just console ourselves with the thought that we had finished reading it anyway!

The sympathetic cat

We have all read about courageous cats, but we do not always know whether these stories are based on the truth. However, having got to know our pet cats, we believe that there *is* probably a great deal of truth in them.

The cat may seem cold, and even a little cantankerous, to those who are unfamiliar with his ways. However, he often demonstrates an amazing sympathy, which can be extremely touching.

The little female cat, who was brought along as a companion for our gray, suffered in silence for a long time, because Memeo, as we have mentioned previously (see *What Did the Cat Say?*), never paid much attention to her. However, she could not bear it when he died, and she searched for him high and low throughout the house, and in all his favorite spots, before she finally gave up, and let herself slip away as well.

Our four-legged friends are extremely aware of our

pain. Our gray cat saw one of his humans crying by herself one day, because she was worried about an operation she had to undergo. He came up to her and sniffed at her face, and gently licked her tears away, before settling down on her lap, glancing up at her occasionally. It was as if to give her comfort, commented the human later. Picò willingly joins in with any discussions the family are having. He will settle himself down amongst us all, and give out his little kisses all around. He cannot bear anyone speaking in an angry tone of voice, or arguments of any kind, but loves laughter. He is always extremely worried when any of 'his' family sneezes, and says "**meow**" as he sniffs at your cold nose. He does not enjoy music, unlike our gray cat, who would sit for hours on your lap as you listened to various operas, sonatas, cavatines or songs. Even Gino Paoli's famous cat used to purr as her musician-human played his guitar.

Helpful advice: There is not much advice we can give here, except to go along with, and encourage, this wonderful side of the cat's nature, and to nurture such long-forgotten feelings in ourselves.

The possessive cat

A cat's property includes the garden, all his things, and even his two-legged companions. Humans think that they own the cat, but they are mistaken. They are actually the sole property of their four-legged friend. He proves this with demonstrations of his affection; curling up on your clothes, settling down on your lap, purring, snuggling up next to you in bed so that he can share your warmth. Unlike the dog, who sits at your feet, the cat has to share the sofa, the armchair, and even your seat at the table.

Each cat has his favorite place, and his favorite human.

Memeo the gray had his 'own' cupboard (see *The guard cat* and *The playful cat*), and also loved to jump up on to the shoulders of anyone who was wearing a dressing gown, having just got out of the bath. He particularly enjoyed rubbing against wet hair.

Sweet little Polly would do anything her two-legged friend asked her to. This was exceptional, but she had suffered at the hands of previous owners, and consequently completely trusted anyone who showed her a little kindness.

Like many other cats, Picò hates the typewriter, the computer keyboard, solitaire playing cards, etc. Anything, in fact, which takes his two-legged friend's attention away from himself.

He is also extremely possessive about his cat biscuits, and even his cat litter.

At one family gathering during the Easter holidays, both Picò and his "cousin-in-law" Paco were in the same house, but kept apart from each other for safety. Paco's human asked Picò's human if she could have some cat litter. This was observed closely by Picò, who reacted by grabbing hold of the bag of litter, snarling and hissing, to make sure it did not get put into a litter tray that did not belong to him. He is usually such a good-natured cat, and this show of possessiveness took us completely by surprise.

Helpful advice: There is not much advice we can give here, either.

1) We leave our cat in peace, even when he is on the sofa. If he is not annoyed about anything, he will remain happy and content for hours. He will not get it dirty because, as we have said many times, the cat is extremely clean.

2) We try to avoid making him jealous, or humiliating him in any way. At the end of the day, he is just another creature who follows his natural instincts.

Adoption of a human

A human never owns a cat, as it is almost inevitably the cat who chooses to live with a two-legged companion. We maintain that he usually does so out of compassion, and never for his own advantage. He will occasionally do so out of necessity.

One morning, outside an extremely popular veterinary surgery in Rome, a young man was desperately trying not to cry, while his girlfriend and another friend tried to console him. We could not help overhearing what they said:

"He never asked for anything, poor little thing. He took shelter in our garden, and wanted to stay there, even though we tried to get rid of him. He was in pain, and we just ignored him. All he wanted was some food and a quiet place to rest. I'm sorry now that I didn't bring him into the house, and I'm sorry we just left him there." Pointing towards the surgery,

he said, "The vet says there's nothing more that can be done for him."

Polly had done the same thing. She was lame, but we never discovered how this had happened, or who had hurt her. Fortunately, she recovered, and repaid us with affection. She was the same little cat who, before the accident, had led one of us to her hiding place, where she had made a cozy nest.

Adopting a human also means educating them. This is where the title of the book comes from. Our four-legged friend actually tries to teach us how to understand his exploits, and how to obey him. As the cat is so clever (see *The intelligent cat*), he easily fits into the human community, absorbing its ideas and ways of living, but not before he has reviewed and corrected them. Or perhaps we should say "uncorrected"?

After dinner, when Memeo got bored, he insisted on going to bed. But he would not go alone. He would only go with his favorite human, whom he dominated completely. She let him get away with this, because he brightened up the dull days, which we all experience, and made them more interesting. (see *The possessive cat*). His companion would instead race around wildly until she was given permission to jump on the bed.

Picò insists on accompanying the oldest of the humans to bed, and then he will come back down and join the rest of us again. Who knows what goes through his little mind. Perhaps he feels he has to accompany all his two-legged companions to bed for the night, one by one, before he can be free to roam around the house at will. If we refuse to go along with him, he will make the most disturbing noises.

The cat will turn to his human when he is unable to resolve a particular problem, recognizing his two-legged companion's superiority. A beautiful black cat, which had been poisoned, came to us for help. We rushed around frantically, looking for a vet, but when we came back the cat had disappeared.

Picò's mother insisted that we should follow her, meowing persistently, trying to tell us that her companion needed help. Fortunately, whilst we were hesitating, wondering whether we had understood where she wanted us to go, and pondering about what we should do if he was on someone else's property, the cat, a big, extremely good-natured creature, suddenly reappeared and, although in a bad way, was able to take some food.

Another female cat, having just given birth to a large litter, could not revive the smallest kitten, and brought him to us for help, in the belief that we would be able to do something. We felt completely useless and stupid.

Owning a cat brings certain responsibilities and obligations.

The cat has particular requirements which he expects his human to fulfil:

1) When he wants to be affectionate, he expects to receive some attention in return, even if his human is in the middle of doing something important which cannot be postponed.

2) But if he wants to be on his own for a while, he expects not to be disturbed.

3) His decision is final, just like the referee's at a football match.

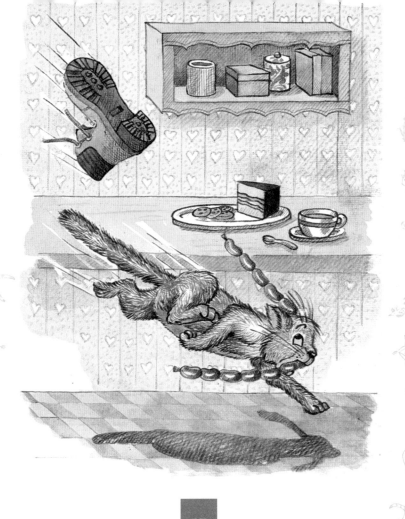

4) If the cat wants to play, his two-legged companion should go along with this.

5) As you do the gardening one sunny morning, remember not to pull up the so-called weeds from the borders, or from the tubs. His Majesty the cat uses this grass to clean his stomach and clear his bowel.

Helpful advice: Who needs advice – our four-legged friend, or his two-legged companion?

The playful cat

The cat is fond of playing games, even when he is getting older and should be settling down a little. There are many toys that you can buy from pet stores for your four-legged friend, such as brightly-colored balls or toy birds and mice.

Right from when he is a kitten, any one of these toys will attract his attention, and lead to merry chases. But it is a ball which fascinates him most of all, even when he is older.

When Picò was small, he enjoyed plucking the toy birds, and chasing around after a ball until it rolled under a cupboard, and someone had to help him retrieve it (see *The intelligent cat*). Our ginger tomcat, having had at least five brothers and sisters, had been used to playing in company, and still enjoys doing so.

Even though he is now eight years old, he still loves playing with a ball, and is overjoyed when he

can draw someone into a game of hide and seek.
The human hides behind a door, where the cat finds
him straight away, and sends him home. The cat will
then swap roles, crouching down behind the same
door, ready to ambush his pursuer's feet. When he
feels like making things more difficult, and livening
up the game, he will crawl under the tablecloth, hide
behind a chair, inside a bag, or under a bed. His
eyes light up, and he is obviously delighted when he
hears his human say:

"Where's Picò?"

He has to hold back the urge to reply:

"**Ahoh ahah ahah**", as he does when he wants
someone who is having trouble finding him to
discover his whereabouts in his secret hiding place.
Instead, he remains very quiet, and only bounds out
when he hears that his pursuer is becoming
impatient, fearful that this wonderful game might be
about to end, calling out victoriously:

"**Aymmah ahoh**".

Hiding himself or some object so as to draw his
two-legged friend, albeit unwillingly, into a game of

hide and seek, is something a cat finds hard to resist. Have you mysteriously lost a pair of socks, as if they had vanished into thin air? Look under the carpet, or beneath your favorite chair, that is if they have not actually been used to cover up the litter tray.

The cat's two-legged friend will occasionally tidy away her CDs, reorganizing her favorite Mina songs, for example, or Gino Paoli, Andrea Bocelli, some Pavarotti, or The Beatles.

She finishes sorting them out, and goes to answer the telephone, or to do some other chore requiring attention. But a loud noise suddenly makes her heart sink. What has that wretched cat gone and done now? He has only knocked the CD holder on to the floor with some carefully aimed blows of his paws, scattering the CDs all over the place. Before his human can catch up with him, the cat has disappeared from the scene of the crime as quick as a flash, and is hiding away somewhere. Why did he do it? To join in the game his two-legged friend was playing, of course, and liven it up a bit!

As we were preparing a meal one day, Memeo grabbed a string of pork sausages and placed them carefully on the bookcase. He just wanted to try out a new game on his two-legged friends. It was precisely because of this playfulness that his human fell in love with him as a kitten, when she saw him playing with a sunbeam on the Spanish Steps in Rome, watched by a group of admiring tourists, and decided that she had to take him home. Despite his size, Memeo used to amaze us with his agility. He learned how to play football with one of our nephews, from the top of 'his' cupboard (see *The guard cat*). The boy would throw a rubber ball, or a piece of screwed-up newspaper, towards him, and the cat would hit it away, just like an experienced goalkeeper. He never used to miss.

It is a good sign if your cat continues to play even as he is getting older. It shows that he is fit and well, and content with life.

Helpful advice: Even if you come home from work feeling tired, your cat will be pleased to see you again and, believing that you are also pleased to see him, he will consider that a brisk run around the garden together is the best way to show how pleased you both are. If you do not have a garden, a brisk jog together along the corridor will suffice. If you do not have a long enough corridor, you can still keep him happy by accompanying him around the table. At a run, of course!

Do you think you can get out of such a wonderful game? Do you want to start a war, by any chance? Tell him so, and your cat will immediately begin sharpening his claws on your jeans, just for starters.

A small hint: if you do not want to be woken up every single night by your cat wanting you to join in with his noisy, boisterous games in the middle of the night, make sure you put your foot down as soon as you get the cat home. Once your four-legged friend has decided that he really likes playing that particular game, it is useless trying to convince him that you want to get to sleep because it is very late, and you need to recharge your batteries. It will be extremely difficult to put a stop to the cat's continuous attempts to include you in his wonderful

game of leaping and jumping around. So what should you do? Firmly shut your obstinate playmate in the bathroom, at least until his desire to play has passed. It will not be easy to calm him down, as he will wake up punctually the following evening, even if he seems to be fast asleep, as if he had a Swiss watch inside his head, ready to play once again. Who will win in the end? Who knows! Joking aside, you will only succeed if you make sure you put a stop to any bad habits as soon as they start, as His Majesty the cat is far easier to control when he is still a kitten.

The intelligent cat

Cats know how to open doors. All right, so dogs can open doors, too. But only medium-size or large dogs can do so, and cats never grow to the same sort of size. So how do they do it? They simply jump up and grab the handle with their front paws. This causes the handle to move downwards, and the door to unlatch and swing ajar. The cat hooks his paw around the door, and opens it all the way. He will generally use his right paw, as 'left-handed' cats are quite unusual.

Picò only has to stretch a little to reach, and does not even need to jump up, as he did when he was a kitten. He can now easily reach the handle, not only because he is quite tall, but also because all the door handles in our flat have been positioned so that a child can reach them. In order to prevent him from leaving the house, or leaving a room in which he has been temporarily shut away for safety (see

Sociable or unsociable?), the human must turn the key in the lock. When Picò sees us doing this, he insolently turns his back on us, and goes as far away as possible. He did once try to turn the key by grasping it between his teeth, but he never did this again, realizing that nothing would ever shift that infernal contraption.

Still on the subject of doors, when Picò starts wailing because he wants to go out on the terrace, or making a fuss because he wants some fresh air, we make sure all the terrace windows are open so that he can get back in if he needs to in a hurry.

A poor little female cat, who ended up in a research laboratory, saved herself from certain death by poisoning from the gas with which they were experimenting, by realizing where the gas was coming into her cage. She blocked the opening with one of her paws as soon as she heard the hissing noise. The cat's intelligence so impressed one of the researchers working in the laboratory that he rescued her.

When he was a kitten, Picò loved to chase after a ball (see *The playful cat*), repeatedly rolling it

underneath a piece of antique furniture, which had a narrow space underneath its four short, solid, round feet. We soon understood why he kept doing this. He had noticed that, on his insistence, one of the humans had used a thin stick, which was usually kept in the umbrella stand, to retrieve the ball. So he thought he could copy this, and attempted to get the stick out of the brass umbrella stand, showing just how clever, and independent, he really could be. So his human changed her tactics. She took out the bottom drawer and reached through the gap to pick the ball up off the floor. The cat could hardly believe it when he realized that he, too, could jump into this gap and knock the ball so that it suddenly shot out from its hiding place. It was no good pointing out that this game could just go on forever. He did grow out of it, however, and eventually turned his attention to other things.

For a short while, Memeo made friends with a large cat called Tarzan, who had some Persian and a few other varieties as well in his breeding. The two of them used to have lots of fun in the garden, chasing moles. They would patiently wait at the end of a tunnel – how they located it was always a source of wonder and amazement to us. One of them to the left, the other to the right, they would wait patiently for the mole to emerge, at which point they would chase after it. Their games were a great help to the plants and trees in the garden, whose roots were continually being threatened by the strong, clawed feet of the little burrowers.

We use the same water bowl for Picò that Memeo used to have, which we fill up with fresh water each morning. We put it on a ceramic tile, though we are not sure whether this is because it looks nice, or whether it keeps it cleaner. Picò drinks a large amount, and there is sometimes very little water left in the bowl, particularly during the night. To get to it more easily, Picò will put his paw in the bowl to see how much is left, and move it to the edge of the tile so that the bowl tilts slightly onto the floor and the water collects at one side, so he can drink more easily.

Just like all cats, Memeo used to get extremely jealous of his territory. He came away with us to our holiday home by the sea on one occasion, and quickly chased away an interloper who had dared to come into 'his' garden. The garden backed right on to the street. The two cats recklessly leapt over the fence, and the human who was chasing after them, trying to make them stop, nearly had apoplexy, at the thought that they were almost certain to be run over in the busy street. The two cats, however, were not that stupid, and although they were both furious, they suddenly came to a standstill. By mutual agreement, one of them climbed back into the garden, and the other turned off to the left.

For a short time, one of our female cats tried to pick a fight with her reflection in the mirror. She looked for the intruder in the wardrobe, managing to climb in while the human was not looking. She soon understood what it was all about, however, and did not even glance at the mirror any more when she walked past it.

One of the male cats managed to pull the alarm cord whilst trying to open the shutters. Once was

enough! The deafening noise scared him so badly that he never went near that fatal cord again.

Picò, yes, him again, whilst he was dreamily curled up on the bathmat, had first-hand experience of the loud, vibrating jacuzzi, which the human had turned on while she was in the bath. Our ginger tom enjoyed curling up at the foot of the bath, as did Memeo, convinced that his very presence would keep his two-legged friend safe, as she recklessly exposed herself to goodness knows what perils. Before this devilish contraption was installed the bath used to be a different shape and the cat thought it was great fun to play a kind of hide and seek with his two-legged companion, he in the dry area, the human completely submerged, except for her nose and mouth. His two-legged companion would call out: "Hey, Picò! Picottinooo."

"**Meooh**?" he would reply. If he felt like it.

"Come here", his human would say sarcastically, punctuating her feline friend's fear of water.

"**Meow, meooow**", the cat would reply, even more sarcastically.

Everything changed when the jacuzzi was installed. What a disturbance for a poor cat, who only wants some peace and quiet, but has to leap up quickly and take refuge between the sink and the bidet, trying to hide from the imminent tidal wave, albeit a small one, but a tidal wave nonetheless.

Picò now refuses to come into the bathroom when his human is in the bath, but watches over her from outside the door.

Helpful advice: 1) You certainly should not give up using the jacuzzi just to please your cat. The best solution is Picò's way of coping with the situation.

2) A sensible, loving, obedient(!) human will always accompany his cat when he wants to go roaming. You should go along with him, not over roofs or along ledges, of course, but following a more practical route. It will do you good, if nothing else. As far as roofs and ledges are concerned, it may be a good idea to put up some netting to prevent access, which even the most agile cat will find impossible to get through, however much he wants to go wandering.

The cat's etiquette

It is well known that Honoré de Balzac, one of the greatest French novelists, was a cat-lover. He had a female cat for a while, whom he taught to eat at the table. He built a special chair, and served the cat with the same meals he ate himself. If his four-legged friend did not finish up all her soup, she did not get served the main course.

It is unknown whether the cat ever rebelled against this. If she did not, then Balzac must have been the only human to have ever won over a cat completely.

However, the cat does favor a certain amount of etiquette at mealtimes. Even the so-called stray cats, whether they are on their own or in a group, who await the kind-hearted women, so often, quite incorrectly and disdainfully called "*gattare*", or "*cat ladies*", to come along with some tempting leftovers. They might be so hungry that they cannot think

straight, but they will always remember to weave around the legs of the person who has brought them some food, a "thank you" rub, emphasized by the customary "**ron ron**".

Female cats make the most impatient pets, and will often be quite ungrateful, barely expressing their gratitude at all. A male cat, however, out of sheer coquetry, or just from a desire to be loved, will sometimes even lower himself to asking to be spoon-fed, just like a baby. In fact, if you allow him to eat the same food as you are eating, he will even let you set a place for him at table. So Balzac's cat was not that unusual. However, it is not a good idea to let your cat join you at the dinner table when you have guests! And not all humans would agree with having an extra place at the table for the cat, even when there are no guests around.

Picò never shares our meals, as he prefers his special cat biscuits, but he does like to sit on a chair by the table with us, where he will curl up and contentedly remain until we have finished.

Except when he is seeking revenge, your four-legged friend will usually let you sleep in peace. And even when you encourage him to accompany you to bed, saying "Come along, it's time to go to sleep", he will follow you, going through the usual rituals in an attempt to allay your suspicions. He will curl up beside you, amicably wriggling his bottom against you and, closing his beautiful eyes, will pretend to fall into a deep slumber. With true feline patience, he will wait until you have really gone to sleep, and will then nimbly leap from the bed in order to do his own thing.

Helpful advice: There would not be any point writing this book if life were really like this. The relationship between you and your cat will usually include many unexpected whims and fancies on his part (see previous chapters), so it is worth getting used to this, as they will always take you by surprise. I tell you this as a fellow cat-owner and admirer.

Good points vs. bad points

We allowed Paco, Picò and Arthur to scrutinize the following list of feline paradoxes, which they agreed with, albeit somewhat doubtfully. The old saying that "the truth is always hardest to swallow" also applies to the cat. But faced with overwhelming evidence, they all had to concede some of the points:

1) patient – obstinate;
2) affectionate – will turn on you suddenly with claws out;
3) unselfish – over-developed sense of possessiveness;
4) wary – foolhardy;
5) cautious – overwhelmingly curious.

Helpful advice: We have no advice to give on these points, as you should draw your own conclusions, based on your own experiences.

Cat hates

Your cat will usually become extremely irritable if he has to wear a collar, whether it has a little bell attached to it, or not. Some vets claim that having to wear a collar with a little bell attached can sometimes cause our four-legged friend to develop a nervous complaint. Many owners, however, believe that they are really useful, as it means they can easily keep an eye on what their cat is up to, and can locate him when he goes missing.

Memeo used to keep his little bell quiet by holding it firmly under his chin. However, having been forced to wear one ever since he was a kitten, he was so accustomed to it that he became quite upset if it was taken off. He soon got over it, however.

When the collar became worn out and had to be replaced, or his human happened to see a really stylish one, he would be shown the new collar, and told, "Come on, let's make you nice and smart." This was the magic phrase. With a resigned "**nyaaah**", Memeo would put up with this insult to his superiority without making any fuss. He probably thought that it was not worth it.

Picò managed to get his first collar off, and to hide it so successfully that it was never ever found.

The cat's second pet hate are curtains or drapes which obscure his view of the street. It is well known that the cat loves to sit for hours at a time on the windowsill, watching dogs walking by beneath him, so the experts claim. If the window is closed, it is quite hard to see outside. Imagine how frustrating it can be if there is a curtain obscuring the view completely. Picò has learned how to pull the curtains down, and also that it is better to beat a hasty retreat from the commotion he has caused.

The cat actively loathes your hairdryer, because it hisses more than he does; and he detests the hairbrush, particularly when you are using it to brush his coat. And, of course, there is his travelling cage. The following should also be included on a list of items disliked by the cat: your computer, your books, newspapers, and the typewriter, which your four-legged friend will stubbornly refuse to ever accept.

Helpful advice: 1) In order to avoid tears in your precious curtains, you should deter the rascal from doing whatever he likes by placing various objects on the windowsill, such as a draft stopper, or anything that would be difficult to move. This will work until your four-legged friend decides that it is time to launch an all-out attack. What can you do then? Not have any curtains at all, or keep the window open and just get used to the cold draughts? No. Sooner or later, the cat will learn that he has to behave himself, and will just stop doing it. It is absolutely true: just try it and see.

2) A collar is indispensable, particularly if you attach a little tag with your cat's name and address on it, as you often see on a dog's collar. This is extremely useful should your cat unfortunately run away or go missing.

3) The cat has to get used to all your things. It is best not to let him get the upper hand, even if this results in many... heated discussions!

The unpredictable cat

They say that, right from the very first drops of rain, to the great flood itself, the cat was not amongst the animals which were gathered together by Noah to go on to the Ark. It appears that God forgot to create the cat. However, when the rain ceased, and the Ark finally grounded on the summit of Mount Ararat, and the gangplank was lowered over the water on to Armenian soil, two unknown creatures trotted out, tails held aloft like periscopes. They were later called Cats. Before they disappeared into the undergrowth with all the other animals, they headed straight for the Patriarch, humbly rubbed against his legs, and took their leave with a gentle "**Meow**". Half astonished, and half amused, the old man thought that the Heavenly Father must have wanted to make up for His forgetfulness. He was well aware that he had been given the responsibility of looking after all these animals, and wanted to find out a little more about the strangers. How had these two creatures been born? He decided that they must have been born on the Ark and must have had an earthly father and mother. His suspicions focused on the monkeys and the lions in whom he had perceived a certain furtiveness. Had the monkey fathered them, or the magnificent lion? It appears that he was never able to prove anything.

This is why the cat is so unique, and differs from all other creatures. He is completely unpredictable, a mixture of pride and cunning, independence and refinement. Memeo had been forced to accept poor, injured Polly as a companion and, during their initial violent scraps, she used to take refuge right on top of our feet whenever he was about to get the better of her. Particularly if one of us was wearing a long dressing-gown, as she could watch from beneath it, and see Memeo's chagrin, as she well knew he would not dare go for her whilst she was safely hidden away there. Hot-tempered Memeo would come to an abrupt halt, aware that he could not reach her there, as crafty Polly had foreseen.

After Polly's first few attempts at sneaking away from

the veterinary surgery, where we took her because she was still so poorly, she finally came to terms with these visits, as long as she could put her head under a human's arm, so that she could not see the white gown which bustled all around her tortured body.

Tarzan could not stand the care his human took of the house, and particularly hated three unusually-shaped, hand-decorated, brightly-painted bottles, which had been carefully arranged on a little table. He used to regularly jump up on to this table, without moving any of the bottles, amongst which he would to sit conspicuously upright, his tail hanging down amongst the folds of the tablecloth. The first day this happened, his human, having searched for him in all the customary places finally discovered him pretending to be a fourth bottle, and jokingly dusted him over. Tarzan just let her carry on, and expected to be dusted every day after that.

Picò always comes when his humans whistle, as if he were a dog, but he ignores the "pss, pss" which people generally use to call cats. There is one big difference between him and a dog, however. A dog will always come when called; Picò will only come when he feels like it. When he does not, he gives voice to his distinctive "**meeaaa**", which means that he is not going to shift himself, and the human will then have to go and find him, and cajole him into doing whatever it is that happens to be so important at that precise moment.

Arthur still does his tightrope act on the clothesline, some fifteen meters above the courtyard, completely ignoring human entreaties.

"You'll fall off one day", they tell him.

"**Ooff**", he replies, insolently.

Helpful advice: When faced with this last scenario, you should seriously consider whether you ought to obey your cat, and just go along with what he wants. What if he really does fall off? We always try our very best to stop him doing it. It is usually advisable not to get too enthralled with your cat's funny little ways, and to always put your foot down firmly when he is likely to put himself in danger. Never let him captivate you completely with his spontaneous exploits, if possible.

A creature of habit

A typical day in the life of a pet cat living in a comfortable home would go something like this:

Six o'clock. If no one shows any signs of waking up, the cat, who knows his companions' commitments, jumps up on to the bed and sniffs at the sleepers, tickling them with his whiskers.

Seven o'clock. One of his two-legged companions finally gets out of bed. The cat greets him warmly, and demands his breakfast with a "**Marammamow**". Not quite fully awake, and wanting a bit of peace, his human puts some food in his bowl, and checks that he has got enough water.

Eight o'clock. Before the bed gets made again, the cat crawls under the covers and has a nice little snooze.

Nine o'clock. Hearing the shutters being opened, the cat leaves his cozy bed and goes out on to the terrace, where he spends some time inspecting the plant pots, looking for a certain kind of greenery which he enjoys eating.

Eleven o'clock. The cat comes back inside, as he finds that the weather is never ideal for staying out too long: it is either raining and cold, or it is too hot and sunny. It is much more comfortable in one of the armchairs.

Twelve o'clock. The cat has a nap.

One o'clock. The cat is still asleep.

Two o'clock. The family are sitting around the table, when His Majesty the cat makes an appearance, stretching and remonstrating.

Three o'clock, Four o'clock, Five o'clock, Six o'clock, Seven o'clock. The cat sleeps.

Eight o'clock. The cat goes to meet his human as he comes back home. He somehow recognizes the sound of his car – it is amazing how he does this – and is now standing by the door, ready to greet his two-legged friend, tail in the air.

Nine o'clock. The cat tries to get the family to play with him before dinner, and also after dinner.

Ten o'clock. He goes along with Grandma when she retires for the evening.

Eleven o'clock. He comes back down and rejoins the rest of the family, but is obliged to go along with them when they go to bed.

Twelve o'clock. The cat sleeps, or rather, snoozes.

One o'clock. Many cats are nocturnal creatures, although fortunately this is not true of all pet cats. If, as sometimes happens, he really wants some human company, he will just walk all over you as you sleep. It is up to you to decide what you should do about this.

Helpful advice: It can be a bit of a problem if your cat is a nocturnal creature. There are many cartoons which illustrate the comical lengths to which some people have gone in order to get a good night's sleep. One simple solution might be to prevent your cat from sleeping during the day, although this is not easy to do. It might be better to shut your cat somewhere in the house far away from the bedroom, ensuring that he has access to food and water. Alternatively, after feeding him up, you could give him lots of cuddles, so that he falls asleep with you.

So what does the cat think?

After many years of living with cats, we believe that we really understand them, and so we would like to try and explain what they think about humans. Here are just a few of their opinions:

Allergy

One of my human's friends says, "I can't have the cat anywhere near me, because I'm allergic to cat hair." So what am I supposed to say? "I'm allergic to you, too." So I keep away from him when I see him.

Power struggle

My human believes there is a continual 'power struggle' between us. Why? Just because I won't move my bottom from his newspaper when I think he's read enough. Because I want more to eat even when he thinks I've eaten enough? What does he know? Why should I move away from the goldfish bowl, just because he shouts at me? He doesn't know anything. He doesn't understand how funny it is to make that stupid fish jump right out of the water, even though I hate getting my paw wet!

Cuddles

I will never refuse a cuddle, and I particularly love being tickled on the sides of my mouth and under my chin. I hate being patted on the head, though, especially by people I don't know, who think they can be friendly with me just because they're friends of my human.

Disappointment

It really upsets me when my human says that I'm a disappointment to him. And it completely breaks my heart when he goes on to say that, had he known what it was going to be like, he would have chosen a dog instead. So he would have preferred a dog, would he? I don't think he realizes how disappointed I am in him.

Speech

I know what this means, as humans just talk and talk. I always try really hard to understand what my human is saying, even when he uses all those long words, because I love him really, and want to please him. But I just wonder what would happen if I tried to communicate with him in pure 'cat talk'?

Retreat

When my human sees me disappearing at the sight of someone I don't know, he always says, "He's a grouchy old cat." It's not true. I leave because I don't like the smell of the newcomer. Moreover, I can't stand him because he can't stand me and because he distracts my human's attention from me. If it's a child, I disappear because I know he'll want to pull my tail, or my ears, and I won't be able to do anything about it. I have a deep respect for children!

Scratching

Okay, so I scratch. I want to be able to have a good scratch whenever I get the urge. No one can stop me, but I realize that it's better to do it when no one's looking. If my human catches me scratching, he always wants to stop me harmlessly enjoying myself. He puts some kind of solution on my neck, right underneath the collar which he makes me wear. Or he puts drops into my ears. Okay, so I don't need to scratch after he's done that, but that's the end of my pleasure, too!

Ha! Ha! Ha

My two-legged friend laughs like this when I get up to mischief, as he calls it. I like it when he really laughs, even though I don't actually think I'm getting up to mischief, it's just that I like playing with him, or fooling around. I really hate it when he mocks me, though. I'll give him "Ha! Ha! Ha!" I simply cannot stand it, and I would gladly scratch him. I do love him, though, and I always forgive him in the end.

Unchangeable

My two-legged friend says, "I like cats because they haven't allowed themselves to be affected by so-called progress, or completely domesticated like the dog. The cat has always been the same, since time immemorial, although he's been worshipped, abused and attacked. He watches us, not from above, but from a faraway world of his own. Isn't that so, my little cat?"

*I look at her. I don't think it's from a faraway world of my own, because we're sitting on the sofa together. I think she's very pretty, and she loves me as well. I move closer to her, and reply, "**Ron ron**".*

"You're making him out to be more than he actually is," says the other human. "He's just another animal, a fascinating animal but nothing more."

"But he's the cleverest one. I'm sure he understands me. Look at him. Don't you think he seems to be following our conversation? You really understand, don't you, little cat? And you agree with me, don't you?"

I haven't actually understood very much, but I reply all the same:

"**Ron ron**", and carry on purring. It's very comfortable, sitting here between them.

La La La

"*La La La*". When he shaves, he sings to himself. She does, too, when she's soaking in the bath, covered with bubbles. I fell in once, when I was messing around on the edge of the bath. Those lovely bubbles smell delicious, so much so that I even tried again, but I waited till she'd emptied the water from the bath, of course, and then I rolled about in the froth that was left on the bottom. She laughed when she saw me do this, and told all her friends about it. "*La La La...*" She has a lovely voice, but he's tone deaf! But why is it that they make me put up with their singing, when they always try to shut me up every time I join in as well? "**Ohohoh**", I pipe up. "Be quiet, pussycat. What's the matter? Are you ill?" Ill, indeed! I only want to join in with the singing.

Pussycat

My two-legged companion calls me pussycat, and I reply to her with a gentle **Meow**. It reminds me of my real mother's voice. How many years ago was that? Too many. My real mother had such a gentle voice, and I keep hearing it again, when I'm feeling a bit sad: "**Meoo meoo meoo**". It was so comforting.

Names

When she calls: "Puss, Pussycat, Little one, Sweetheart", I know she means me. She uses loads of names and endearments for me. But I'm a cat, just like any other cat. I also recognize the names of other four-legged and two-legged creatures, from the dog to the horse, to the bird and the chick. I even know that the strange black-feathered creature which says "Hello. Who's that? Go, Lazio!" is called Brutus. I understand that "outside" means the garden or terrace, and that "inside" means anywhere in the house.

My two-legged friend really admires me, and will always stick up for me: "This wonderful cat

understands me, but I'm so stupid that often I don't
understand him."

Pride

My two-legged friend says I'm extremely proud, and
she loves me for this. As far as I can understand, I
apparently look proud when I stalk off with my tail in
the air, refusing any longer to try and make her do
something she doesn't want to do. She's very
stubborn. I'm arrogant because I just stop trying and
walk away, refusing to come running when food is
put in the dish, or to jump up on to her lap for a bit of
fussing when she pats her knee. It's not arrogance. I
just want her to obey me.

Possessions

I am mine. Possessions? Of course, I know what
that means, and go along with the idea. The human
at home is mine, even though he tries to persuade me
that it's the other way round. The house is mine, of
course, and the garden (or terrace), the sofa, the best

carpet, the bed I allow my human to use every night, and the clothes on which I enjoy curling up.

Here

"Come here, pussycat", my two-legged friend calls, expecting to see me come running over, wagging my tail like a dog, pleased to do his bidding, even though I was enjoying the warm sunshine on a lovely spring day. "Come here."

Even though I know he won't give up, I reply: **"Marrammama"**. "Leave him alone," says the female human, "didn't you hear what he just said?"

Nuisance

Yet another name I get called, whenever I try to make him empty the litter-tray; when I want to go to bed, and he wants to watch television; when I don't want to get into the travelling basket; when she has to wake me up because I've snuggled into a warm place, and she wants to make the bed. I just want to reply to both of them: **"Ahmmahmmow"**.

Feelings

My owner desperately tries to prove that I'm actually fond of him, and not the house, as many misguided people believe. They're just not looking deep enough, and merely take things at face value. They mistake my self-restraint for a lack of affection, foolishly thinking that I must have a heart of stone, just because I don't make a big fuss over my two-legged companion when there are other people around. I'd just like to remind these superficial beings that it's always been humans themselves who go on about feline unselfishness and sensibility, of which I can give you many examples.

Puss in Boots is just one of them. He stood up for his poor master, even confronting the wicked ogre, and thus bestowing on his young friend love, riches and happiness.

The cat who taught the seagull how to fly is another good example.

And then there's the cat who called for help. But not for himself.

Another example of unselfishness is the cat who made friends with the cardinal. In case you've forgotten the story, the cardinal was a kind little bird, whose death my fellow creature avenged and thus solved a crime.

And what about the cat with the black patch on her nose, who purred whenever her human played his guitar?

What's that you're trying to tell me? What have I got to say about the cat who belonged to Cinderella's stepmother? Oof! Don't be so pedantic! "**Cahcchcahcch**".

Stubborn

She never says: "How stubborn you are!" Instead, she says: "Well, aren't you the bossy one!"

I reply: "**Ahrrooa**".

Amazingly, she seems to have got the message and says: "So you want to do as you please? Well, I won't give you anything to eat, then."

Oh well, I wasn't hungry, anyway.

Claws

This is a sore subject. My Achilles' heel, as he would say. He tells me that I'm just doing it to annoy him when I scratch the carpet, the chair, the armchair, etc. But that's not strictly true. I really need to do it. And it gives me pleasure. "What an ungrateful hooligan", he shouts when he sees what I'm doing. "One of these days, I'll cut off all of those claws of yours." Deep down, I know that his scolding is just for show. He'll never really carry out his threat. Anyway, I roll over on to my back just to pacify him, and also because I really don't want my claws cut off!

Whiskers

I like to poke my whiskers into everything. I really hate it when I lose a whisker. They seem to grow back ever so slowly, and I feel completely naked.

Bzz bzz

This noise drives me mad until I find out where it's coming from. It might be a mosquito, a bluebottle, or maybe a wasp. So I give chase, stunning it by jumping up and lashing out at it with my paws, until I manage to trap it beneath the curtain and finish it off.

But my two-legged friend is never grateful to me for getting rid of such nuisances, and saving her from possible danger. She gets annoyed with me instead, for having pulled the curtains down, or getting squashed insect all over them.

Helpful advice: Yes, even I would like to give you some helpful advice. Just treat each cat as an individual. Don't try and make him do things he doesn't want to do, or that he doesn't see the point of doing. Let the dog be obedient and obliging. Why should you expect the cat to be the same? The world is a much better place because we're all different, as they say.

Conclusion

You will probably have noticed that there was no chapter entitled *The obedient cat*. To begin with, it would have gone completely against the original intent and purpose for which this little book was written. We have tried to show that, if you really want to become friends with your cat, it can be relatively easy, and often amusing, to go along with what he wants, even if he is disobedient. It is wonderful to see an affectionate relationship developing between a cat and its two-legged friend. Not to mention how fulfilling and pleasing it can be.

However, we hope that it does not stir up the age-old debate about the somewhat shameful tendency that some well-meaning people have to 'humanize' their pet cat. And not just the cat.

Every living thing – including plants, which undergo what is ostentatiously known as "cultivation" but is really nothing more than human manipulation – has the right to grow and develop as nature intends. Just because we have surrendered to progress, do plants and animals have to do so too? A trouble shared is a trouble halved, as they say.

Index

....
....
....
....
....
....
....
....
....
....
....
....